WHAT ... . :

WHAT A WAG!

AN ANTHROPOMORPHIC
A TO Z OF DOGS

Companion Volume to *Tails You Win*

In original verse by
Gill Rowe

Line drawings by Jennifer Taggart

The Book Guild Ltd

First published in Great Britain in 2021 by
The Book Guild Ltd
9 Priory Business Park
Wistow Road, Kibworth
Leicestershire, LE8 0RX
Freephone: 0800 999 2982
www.bookguild.co.uk
Email: info@bookguild.co.uk
Twitter: @bookguild

Typeset in Garamond Premier Pro

Printed and bound in the UK by TJ Books Limited, Padstow, Cornwall

ISBN 978 1913551 346

British Library Cataloguing in Publication Data.
A catalogue record for this book is available from the British Library.

For

Georgia, Daisy, Iona, Rosie and Sebastian

Acknowledgements

With grateful thanks to Tom Stacey for reading the manuscript, Robin Nott for his advice, Jenny Taggart for her lovely line drawings, Charles for his invaluable input and, above all, to Clive for his unfailing encouragement and support.

Contents

Prologue   xi

Alaskan Malamute   1

Alsatian   3

Australian Kelpie   4

Bedlington Terrier   6

Bichon Frise   9

Bloodhound   10

Border Terrier   12

Cavalier King Charles Spaniel   13

Cavpoo   15

Chesapeake Bay Retriever   16

Chihuahua   18

Chow Chow   20

Collie   22

Dandie Dinmont   24

Doberman Pinscher   25

English Foxhound   26

Flatcoated Retriever   29

German Shepherd   31

German Spitz   32

Great Dane   35

Greyhound   36

Harrier   38

Irish Setter   40

Irish Water Spaniel   42

Jack Russell Terrier   44

Japanese Chin   46

Jura Lafhound   47

Kerry Blue Terrier   50

Labrador   53

Lakeland Terrier   56

Leonberger   58

Lurcher   59

Maltese   61

Mastiff   63

Miniature Poodle   64

Newfoundland   67

Norfolk Terrier   68

Otterhound   69

Pomeranian   71

Pomski   72

Rottweiler   73

St. Bernard   75

Saluki   77

Schnautzer   80

Sealyham Terrier   82

Siberian Husky   84

Springer Spaniel   86

Staffordshire Bull Terrier   88

Tyrolean Hound   90

Victorian Bulldog   91

Weimaraner   92

Welsh Corgi   93

Whippet   96

Xolocuintal   98

Yorkshire Terrier   99

Zuchon   100

Postscript   103

Other Works by Gill Rowe   105

Prologue

If, by chance, you don't know about dogs
Never fear, for you'll learn from these pages.

Please give yourself time to enjoy the odd
rhyme,
Revealing that canines are sages.
And you'll find an amazing array,
It's astonishing how varied they are.
Since all are descended from wolves,
Expect some echoes of howls from afar,

Or, if you've always had dogs in your life,
Forgive the omissions, for many there are.

Dogs are our mentors; they teach by
example.
Of their wisdom we learn every day.
Grumble, they won't. Nor judge. They just
love.
So read on, and imbibe what they say.

Alaskan Malamute

I am the Mr. Strong of dogs.
I am full of vim and verve.
I can pull enormous loads.
My calling is to serve.

I do not run as speedily
As the Siberian Husky.
We look alike, but I'm heavier,
And his colouring is dusky.

We both wear heavy double coats,
Our magnificent tails coil back.
But I take the prize for hauling loads;
Of my accolades I've lost track.

Fifteen hundred kilograms
Have been loaded on my sled.
You cannot fail to be impressed.
'Twas for this that I was bred.

Today, hauling for me is *passé*;
Machines are used for it all.
I'm now a much-loved family pet.
I've retired, and life's a ball!

Alsatian

My breed was born from xenophobia.
I was given my name after World War 1,
When anything German came in for hate –
'German Shepherd' recalling 'The Hun'.

It is derived from the French name, *Alsace*,
Which betokened our solidarity.
This new, classy name quite suited me.
As for features, there's no disparity.

I loved my short life as an Alsatian.
I am sad that my time has been ended.
But, it must be said, though officially dead,
I am constantly being befriended.

Australian Kelpie

I'm a master herder;
Give me flocks or herds,
I'll drive them with *panache*,
Without the use of words.

My origins are 'Strine',
But everywhere I please
Farmers who feel the need
Of my skill and expertise.

My stature – I stand tall –
Exudes authority.
Quick thinking is, of course,
The real priority.

My pointed ears are pricked.
My hearing is acute.
Though I'm quite a looker,
Don't ever call me cute!

For I'm a working dog,
Proud of my profession.
I'm bright, I'm keen, I'm fast,
But my best possession

Is that of second sight
With animals I tend;
They do not resent me.
I treat them as my friend.

The colour of my coat,
Which is both smooth and short,
Ranges from brown to gold.
Sprinting is my best sport.

Now that you know about me,
You will see me when you roam
Down Under and the wider world.
Were you to take me home,

You would find me very friendly.
With the young I get on fine,
But since I herd, I might one day
Put your children in a line!

Bedlington Terrier

My close-cut woolly coat and snout-less
    pear-shaped head
Have suggested to some people a likeness
    to a lamb.
This patronising notion has caused me
    great offence.
No terrier can be sheep like; the whole
    idea's a sham.

Though my curious delineation may make
    me look fragile,
My history and experience show absolutely
    the reverse;
I've killed rats for miners and been friend
    to poachers.
Folk once called me 'gypsy dog' for stealing
    and for worse.

Yet with the passing years, my life has
    been refined.
For with the changing times I have
    modified my style.
I am still as feisty, speedy and courageous,
But I have been a cuddly dog for quite a
    little while.

Yes, I have learned the manners of the
    drawing room.
I have long been converted to comfort,
    warmth and ease.
I can make myself appear to be a soft and
    woolly toy.
Let me curl up on your lap and I'll be
    guaranteed to please.

Bichon Frise

I'm a pure white bundle of fluff.
I resemble a powder puff.
I am light on my toes,
I've a shiny black nose,
Of attention I can't have enough.

I was once a favourite at court.
But when that charmed life was cut short,
I went out in the sticks
To learn circus tricks.
I know more than you'd ever have thought.

For my brain is sharp as a knife.
I avoid all tension and strife,
So I bounce through the day
Always ready to play.
I enjoy every day of my life.

Bloodhound

I've been invited to retire.
I am old, as you would see.
But I'll not abandon sleuthing;
It's the only life for me.

My nose is like a computer;
It identifies, stores and files
The data about criminals.
The print-out would run for miles!

I can't say how many villains
Have been caught because of me.
My police work's quite invaluable,
But they get it all for free.

I have trained up several hound-lets
By teaching them all I knew,
Not least, handling their 'handlers',
Of whom I have met a few.

I am happiest when I'm working,
Head down and nose to the ground.
Years of successful sleuthing
Ensured this hound is renowned.

Border Terrier

My face is reminiscent of an otter's;
Slightly flattened nose and dark brown eye.
But though certainly I don't object to water,
I am happiest with moorland and wide sky.

I'm a wiry coated, smallish brindle terrier
(Though some patches, like my nose, are
    coloured black).
I have the fighting instinct of all terriers;
It is I who often goes on the attack.

Originally, I'm from the Scottish Borders,
It's not surprising that I am both brave
    and strong.
But you'll see that when we meet, I am
    delightful.
I challenge anyone to say that I am wrong!

Cavalier King Charles Spaniel

I'm going on my holiday.
My tartan bag is packed.
I've got my medication.
The grip's with titbits stacked.

I'm told that I will like the place,
But I really have to say
I don't enjoy the change of scene
When we all go away.

I never want to go abroad,
It spoils my daily routine.
I only go along with it
Because my pets are keen.

I miss my large palatial bed;
The travelling version's bad.
It's thin and lumpy. I don't sleep,
Which really drives me mad.

There are some compensations;
New smells, perhaps new friends.
But, always, I look forward to
The day the holiday ends.

Just in case you're wondering,
Though it's really by the by,
I'm a Cavalier King Charles
Spaniel; a Tri-colour, or Tri.

Cavpoo

I am a fashionable Cavpoo.
Me, I'm more Poo than Cav.,
But whatever the generation,
We're this year's dog 'must have'.

Whether seen in Kensington Gardens,
That most elegant royal park,
Or cavorting along a Cornish beach,
I'm always up for a lark.

I am playful, intelligent, pretty.
What more could you possibly need?
Why, of course! How could I forget it?
My remarkable turn of speed!

Chesapeake Bay Retriever

I trace my origins to a shipwreck,
More than two hundred years back from
    today,
When a ship went down off the coast of
    Maryland,
In the icy waters of Chesapeake Bay.

Two puppies were among the survivors,
Both, fittingly, of the Newfoundland breed.
When grown up, they both wanted to
    marry
Two local retrievers, whose families agreed.

Out of these unions a new breed was born,
Unique of its kind, with the Chesapeake
    name.
I can spend hours in rough, freezing water.
No other canine can do quite the same.

I retrieved hundreds of ducks for the men
Who used to go hunting there, back in
the day.
My thick oily coat still affords me
protection.
I'm the Retriever from Chesapeake Bay.

Chihuahua

I'm a pocket size Chihuahua.
I am very highly bred.
I'm not everyone's cup of tea
'Cos my eyes pop out of my head.

The pygmy of all canine breeds,
My scamper's quick and short.
My hair is smooth, my torso lean.
I yap more than I ought.

I am fearfully energetic,
I could run around all day.
But you'll often see me on a lead,
Which gives no chance to play.

All those who get to know me
Attest that I'm loving and sweet.
Also, because I'm so tiny,
I don't need masses to eat!

Chow Chow

My ancestors are Chinese,
From two thousand years ago.
An ancient civilisation,
As everyone should know.

I am large, hirsute, and golden,
I have a magnificent ruff.
My posterior, too, is impressive,
A contention you can't rebuff,

For my tail is quite enormous.
It curls sturdily over my back,
Showing a paler shade of gold.
I'm immune to any attack.

It's only a few hundred years
Since my kin arrived over here.
When first seen, because of my size,
Folk thought I was someone to fear.

I resemble the king of beasts;
My head's certainly leonine.
But when you examine my face,
You will see that I'm quite benign.

Collie

If you've ever seen me working,
You'll know that I am clever.
But do you know that I've been
Sculpted and so will live for ever
By blue Lake Tekapo's rocky shore,
In New Zealand's southern isle?
When I think of this bronze monument,
It always makes me smile.

For without the humble Collie dog,
Brought over from places like Fife,
The Scottish settlers in New Zealand
Could never have made a life.
Their sheep grazed on hundreds of acres;
They could not have managed at all
Without their faithful, brain-sharp dogs,
Ever there to respond to their call.

We're proud of the special relationship
We have with our shepherd pets.
We understand their every command.
This work is as good as it gets.
I love speeding off to fetch the sheep.
It's fun bringing them back to the pen.
We know when to crouch, and when to
     nudge.
How we do is beyond human ken.

Dandie Dinmont

I am a terrier, but very unusual.
I've a long, curved back and masses of hair.
I have extraordinary round, hazel eyes.
I exude a serene and amiable air.
I am very low-slung. My legs are short.
But my smart top-knot adds to my height.
It's rare, now, to meet Dandie Dinmonts.
If you do, you're in for a beautiful sight!

Doberman Pinscher

I am fearless, and I witnessed scenes
That would curdle your blood, in the war.
Mascot to American Marines,
I'm part Rottweiler, Pinscher and more.

I was bred as a watchdog and guard.
I'll defend to the limit my patch,
Whether orchard, house, garden or yard.
When on duty, for me there's no match.

I'd advise you to be circumspect,
When encountering dogs of my breed.
It is wise to afford me respect.
I am awesome. So do please take heed.

English Foxhound

I really belong in the hunting field.
My galloping skills are renowned.
Using my nose, I hunt in a pack.
I'm a beautiful English Foxhound.

My short coat is white with smart markings;
I've patches of black, brown and tan.
I express my good humour by waving my tail,
Even when squashed in the kennels' old van.

There's nothing to beat the excitement
Of following quarry at speed.
Eagerly baying, we pick up the scent.
I am proud to be one of my breed.

Ruby, Rollo, Rory, Rachel and Rob,
When young, we were all 'walked' together;
Kind people, who love and support our hunt,
Took us daily, whatever the weather.

When not in the field, I am gentle.
I'm amiable, calm and serene.
You would find me a lovable pet;
I am biddable, willing and clean.

But I have to say that my real love
Is covering mile after mile.
So, if given lashings of exercise,
I'll always reward with a smile.

Flatcoated Retriever

I'm an old Flatcoated Retriever.
Though now retired from any sport,
I still do a bit of retrieving,
(Much more, really, than I ought).
When I'm in pole position
Under the dining room table,
I may look quite half-asleep,
But I am more than able
To hoover up tasty morsels
Falling, manna-like, from above.
For me, each day is a field day;
There's almost no food I don't love.

Greek cuisine is the exception.
Dolmades leave me cold and
Tarama's a vile confection!
Perhaps because I'm old,
I love traditional dishes;
I am partial to a roast.

I'm keen on eggs and bacon.
I love my buttered toast.
Best of all is children's tea-time,
When veritably showers
Of tasty treats come tumbling down.
Better still, it lasts for hours!

I've had a wonderful life.
My pets couldn't have been better.
They've bought me a young companion;
A dear little boy Red Setter.
I'm teaching him all I've learned
In my ninety-one years in clover,
So when, finally, I go to sleep,
There'll be someone to take over.

German Shepherd

My name has been restored.
'Alsatian' I deplored.
I had been quite ignored,
Poor German Shepherd Dog.

They took my name away.
Back in the war-torn day
People chose not to say
'The German Shepherd Dog'.

They gave me a French name,
From Alsace. It was a shame.
In Germany I'd won fame.
How could I be a Frog?

But I became inured;
The insult I endured.
Now, justice I've procured
For the German Shepherd Dog.

German Spitz

You'll see I wear a handsome ruff.
I'd look good in doublet and hose;
With my narrow ankles and slender
Legs, I would strike an elegant pose.

But even without the costume,
I always cut quite a dash.
I've a noble and upright deportment.
I could see myself wearing a sash.

You can tell that I'm superior
To many other canine breeds.
But though I may command respect,
I don't have many special needs.

Of course, I need hours of grooming.
I demand a capacious bed.
But I couldn't be more obliging,
As long as you keep me well fed.

My coat is thick, a beautiful cream,
Some cousins are tan, brown or white.
My tail, which is massively fluffy,
Curls over my back. Quite a sight!

My sharp ears are pricked, I wear a smile.
My eyes are a darkish brown.
Who am I? A fine German Spitz;
The handsomest dog about town.

Great Dane

I hold the record for altitude,
Nearly four feet from shoulder to paw.
I'm always the tallest of all my dog cousins.
Some canines live close to the floor.

My nose is Roman. I am imposing.
We come in all colours. I'm black.
My ears are sometimes made to stand up.
Left alone, they are floppy and slack.

I'm glad that our name contains 'Great'.
'Alexander', I'd like to have been called.
When my owner instead named me 'Sooty',
I confess I was, frankly, appalled.

For it couldn't be less appropriate.
Remember that puppet, shown on TV?
Could you think of a much greater contrast
'Twixt that diminutive object and me!

Greyhound

I'm Lyn.
Lean, spare and thin,
Bones showing through my skin.
I strain, in common with my kin,
To win.

I need
To run at speed.
I thought we had agreed
That you would never use a lead.
Take heed.

Once freed,
Let off the lead,
How I relish the speed.
Speed, it must surely be agreed,
I need.

I'm free!
You heard my plea.
Now it is plain to see
What a true Greyhound needs to be;
That's me.

Harrier

I am uncommon and *recherché*.
You may not have heard of me,
For my breed of hound is special;
Very pretty, as all agree.

My colouring and smooth coat
You will all know quite well –
Think Bloodhound, Beagle, Basset –
But of the hound clan, I'm the *belle*.

I come from an ancient lineage;
For hunting my kin were bred.
So I need masses of exercise,
Without which I'd rather be dead.

There is something you should know,
If I am to become your pet;
I may bark or howl if I'm left alone.
Life in a pack, I can't forget.

But I'm an asset to any family;
I'm adaptable, playful and fun.
Halfway between Beagle and Foxhound,
I am a Harrier. Number One!

Irish Setter

My very favourite walk is through this
    beechwood.
It always has some messages for me,
Left by all my canine friends who use this
    footpath.
Here, we're never on the lead but all romp
    free.

Last week, I met another Irish Setter,
Whose colouring and perfume were divine.
We snatched only a few moments of
    conversation.
But I'm hopeful that one day I'll make her
    mine.

The problem is how to ensure our
    meeting;
We shall somehow have to synchronise
    our walks.
She tells me that she's very often brought
    here.
I'm looking forward to having many little
    talks.

∽

Just occasionally, my owners are annoying,
When they pay no attention to what I say.
I make it plain enough when I'm ready for
    a walk,
But there is often a quite unnecessary delay.

I give them every signal I can think of
When I just *know* that my quarry's in the
    wood.
But they, obtusely, think that I am asking
    to be fed.
How I hate it when I am misunderstood!

Irish Water Spaniel

When I was out swimming, the other day,
I met a large frog who asked me to play.
I'd never before encountered a frog –
Odd, in this haven of water and bog.

The frog was very intrigued by my coat;
Liver coloured in hue (*foncé* when I float).
I am proud of its masses of tightly coiled
    curls;
When wet, in the sun, they glimmer like
    pearls.

I did not fancy his smooth, mottled skin.
To me it looked strange, and horribly thin.
But he was charming. We got on a treat
As soon as we found we both have webbed
    feet.

Jack Russell Terrier

Limping home, from breaching the peace
    tonight –
'Twas my assailant who started the fight –
I caught sight of myself and it gave me a
    fright;
I'd scratches and bruises, one eye shut tight.

I knew when I left I'd been in the wars;
I felt battered and bruised right down to
    my paws.
I'd not wanted to fight. He was really the
    cause
Of this brawl, but it won me applause.

It is true that I had called him 'young squirt'.
He had gone beyond the pale; he'd dished
    up dirt
Concerning me and that nasty little flirt
From The Fox and Hounds. I left him quite
    inert.

He'll not bother me again, of that I'm sure,
For after this, he's bound to know the score.
But my victory's really cost me; I am sore.
I'm going home to nurse my damaged paw.

Japanese Chin

I am an elegant prima donna.
I move with a graceful, high stepping gait.
By the Japanese court I was favoured.
You should know that I'm used to high estate.

But despite my imperial past I am fun;
I'm skittish and playful all of the time,
Until, quite exhausted, I flop on the floor.
When to disturb me would be a great crime.

I need skilful and regular grooming,
For my silky hair growth is prolific.
But once the plume of my tail has been fixed,
My appearance is truly terrific.

Jura Lafhound

I'm related, though not closely, to the
    Bloodhound.
You may see a likeness in my wrinkled face.
We do share some other salient features,
But I come from a very different place.

My home is in the Jura, on the French
    Swiss border.
Over my domain the Jura Mountains tower.
Here, I am in my element. This is what I'm
    bred for:
I love to hunt. I've stamina and power.

My thick legs are shortish, my body is strong.
I was trained to hunt fox, hare and even small
    deer.
I may look alluring but don't be deceived.
I could never be anyone's pet. No fear!

I'm bred for this life. I love Jura's wild
    landscape.
I could not survive in a city or town.
My role is to hunt in these rugged wild
    places.
This is my calling, for which I wear the
    crown.

Don't listen to him.
The chances were slim
That I'd become prim,
Soft as foam.

I used to hunt game
(I've 'hound' in my name).
Now, still made the same,
I stay home.

I've a large wrinkly face.
I set a good pace
When having a chase,
If I roam.

But I'm not around.
For this Jura Lafhound,
Me, I've gone to ground.
I stay home.

I'm a family pet,
The best you could get.
You've not seen me yet
When at home.

Kerry Blue Terrier

I've a spring in my step and a twinkling eye,
I'm jocular, charming and merry.
My thick coat's a blue
Of astonishing hue,
I'm a terrier, from fair County Kerry.

My unique appearance is dashing and
    fetching;
Girls all fall for my charms like flies.
I may give them a song,
But will never stay long,
For I value the gift of surprise.

You won't, anywhere, find another like me –
The skill of my barber has made sure of that.
My moustachioed face,
Though commanding, has grace.
I'd also look good with a cane and a hat,

For I'm light on my feet. I'm so nimble,
You'll not catch me. I'll lead you a dance.
My favourite gig
Is a fine Irish jig.
Try it, if ever you're given the chance!

You are very unlikely to meet me abroad;
I rarely stray far from the Emerald Isle.
But, were you to come,
To my charms you'd
    succumb,
When met by my warm Irish smile.

Labrador

I expect you will all have seen me
When you have been out and about.
I've been trained to care for my blind pet.
I'm the one he can't be without.

I can tell him when he should cross the road,
I help him to climb up the stairs.
He is never without me by his side,
So nothing takes him unawares.

Me, I've been trained as a carer;
I learned different skills that way.
I pick up mail, open the fridge.
I love my work. I relish each day.

I am needed, valued, cherished, loved.
Without me, my charge couldn't survive;
I've changed his life which before was grim.
Now he rejoices in being alive.

My name is Tab,
A yellow Lab.,
The deepest golden version, as you see.
But though my hair
Is thick and fair,
That's not all that you should know about
	me.

My eyes are dark.
They have a spark,
Particularly, should you be offering me
A little treat.
Whether sour or sweet,
I'll devour whatever tasty food I see.

My paw is large.
Like a small barge.
I leave a trail of massive prints after me.
Back from the walk,
After our talk,
You'll find me well and truly ready for my tea.

Lakeland Terrier

I may appear to be pleased with myself,
Some people have called me 'bold'.
I stand proud and straight. And it's certainly
True I don't like to do as I'm told.

For I am a terrier, through and through.
I am bright, quick-witted and tough.
Sometimes, it seems, I may pander to you,
But I'll let you know when I've had
    enough.

My tightly curled coat is black and tan.
My square jaw shows firmness and strength.
My straight legs are strong, as is my bark.
When on guard, I will go to quite any length.

I am proud of the place that I come from,
With its beautiful mountains and lakes.
Simply nowhere can rival its beauty.
When leaving The Lakes, my heart breaks.

That shows that I do have a softer side.
I might curl up beside you at night.
But when I meet dogs, all that will vanish;
There is nothing to beat a good fight.

Leonberger

It is said that I was bred to be symbolic
Of the lion in Leonberg's coat of arms.
In case you've never met a Leonberger,
Let me describe my considerable charms.

First of all, I have a magnificent head,
Thick hair, dark eyes and huge padded paws.
It's not just my looks that will impress you.
Round the world, my temperament wins
    me applause.

For although it is true I resemble a lion,
There is nothing whatever cruel about me.
I'm gentle. I'm playful. I'll give you a kiss.
Try stroking my ruff and you'll see.

Lurcher

I was the first designer dog,
Though not recognised as such.
It is true that I lack glamour;
My features don't amount to much.

No, mine is known as a cross breed,
Which never gets recognition,
Or registered with the Kennel Club.
I've been cast into perdition.

One parent is always a sight hound,
Its mate from a terrier line.
Lurcher, my name, is not sexy,
But I think it suits me just fine.

I am fleet of foot, like one parent,
Strong and feisty, like the other.
I was once called 'the poachers' friend'.
I lived with them like a brother.

The latest smart designer dogs
Were bred with 'cute factor' in mind,
You will see them everywhere you go.
About us, some views are unkind.

My bony back, which is long and arched,
Is wiry-coated. Mine is grey.
I may not now be *à la mode*,
But Lurchers will yet have their day.

Maltese

Oh my, how beautiful I am!
My coat is a canine dream;
Thick, lustrous, soft as cotton wool,
The colour of Jersey cream.

My ears are small and neat,
I've a pert, *retroussé* nose.
I'm elegant from the coif of my hair
To the tips of my fluffy toes.

My eyes are soft as velvet,
A beautiful Vandyke brown.
My style is aloof and regal,
But I very rarely frown.

For I am sociable and fun,
Despite my superior air.
People fall in love with me.
I know life isn't fair;

My looks give me advantages
Over most breeds in the book.
I am showered with affection
Because of how I look.

Far be it from me to boast,
But it has been said of me –
I'm a sweet Maltese – that my breed
Is the prettiest you will see.

Mastiff

I'm one of the largest dogs on this earth.
My square head and paws are massive.
My history goes back hundreds of years.
Throughout, I have been far from passive.

I am a hunter, guard dog, and trooper.
I'm no stranger to blood sports; I've fought
My own kind, bear, boar and the lion
In the name of legitimate sport.

That gives a hint of how powerful I am,
My strong muscles ripple under my skin.
My low-slung, long tail coils up at the end.
With me on your side, you will win!

Miniature Poodle

I'm bouncy. I'm happy. I'd say!
The dawn of each cracking new day
I greet with delight.
Morale high as a kite,
I'm itching to go out and play.

I'm also incredibly cute.
About this, there can be no dispute.
My eyes are alight.
My muscles are tight.
Yes, I'm an absolute beaut..

I am endlessly cheerful, upbeat.
For each stranger, or friend, that I meet
I wag my smart tail,
Which never does fail
To make humans remark that I'm 'sweet'.

But that is not all I can do;
Dressed up in my cheerful frou-frou,
I do circus tricks,
From which I get kicks.
This career I am keen to pursue.

Newfoundland

I am known to be highly intelligent.
I get on well with the human race.
Despite my quite gargantuan size,
I fit in; I never look out of place.

With Alice and family I go to the seaside,
Where my life saving skills are renowned.
I've gone to the rescue of many a child.
Without me, they might have been
    drowned.

For I am a water baby at heart.
I came here from Canada's eastern shore.
I was, for many years, a working dog,
But I don't really work anymore.

I am very laid back. I like to relax.
I don't have an ounce of malice.
But if needed, I will be up in a trice,
To rescue dear little girls like Alice.

Norfolk Terrier

Please don't confuse me with my Norwich
    cousin.
It's true that superficially we look alike,
But while my silky ear flops engagingly,
His points to the sky and ends in a spike.

We both have thick coats, brindle in colour,
Smart cut off trousers and sparky brown eyes.
But he's happiest in his cathedral city.
I relate more to my county's wide skies.

I was bred to hunt for small vermin,
I've lost count of the numbers that I put
    away,
But now that you find me as somebody's pet,
I'd still catch a mouse, but only to play!

Otterhound

I am a very unusual hound;
I have webbed feet, and a thick shaggy coat.
My woolly ears tumble right over my ears,
Except when I'm having a bit of a float.

Water is really my spiritual home;
I delight in swimming, diving and all.
I love shaking great showers over my pet
When returning to land, on hearing his call.

I was bred, trained and used to hunt otters;
This fine profession unique to my breed.
But now that otters are fully protected,
My special skills have rather gone to seed.

Pomeranian

I'm known for my ruff and feathery trousers.
Also, for my quite exuberant tail.
It lies flat, and fans out on my back.
My thick coat spreads out like a sail.

I was once favoured by monarchs.
That endorsement had made me star.
Sure, I am small, but they call me a toy,
Which is taking the thing a bit far.

For I am not merely a plaything,
There is serious work to be done.
I am taken to shows, where I triumph;
I've lost count of the cups I have won.

Pomski

You may never have made my acquaintance;
My stellar breeding ensures I'm quite rare.
With palest blue eyes and silver-grey fur,
My style is suggestive of long hours of care.
Just look at my truly magnificent tail,
Which curls fluffily over my back.
In the wind it resembles a mainsail,
But it's never allowed to go slack.

My background is truly designer:
One half Pomeranian, Huskie the other.
I'm particularly proud of my fine ruff,
Which I get from my glamorous mother.
I like living in those smart apartments.
I prefer carpets with luscious soft pile.
I am always indulged. I'm persuasive;
Give me an inch and I'll take a long mile!

Rottweiler

I find any food delicious.
I can't say that I'm judicious
About whether it's nutritious.
I'm a Rottweiler.

The rumours that I'm vicious
Are really quite fictitious.
Often people are malicious.
I'm a Rottweiler.

My behaviour is audacious,
My appetite voracious,
My character tenacious.
I'm a Rottweiler.

My press has been pernicious.
It makes people superstitious.
But please don't be suspicious.
I'm a Rottweiler.

For the omens are auspicious.
This may strike you as capricious;
A guru told me it's propitious
To be a Rottweiler.

St. Bernard

When people think of me, they often think
    of brandy,
For I'm usually depicted wearing a small cask,
Which I carry up the mountains to revive
    the poor wretches
Who have come to grief. How I relish this
    task.

I am the epitome of a gentle giant.
I've a massive build and a quite enormous
    head.
Imagine the joy when I sniff out and approach
Injured climbers who might, without me, be
    dead.

Originally, I was guard dog to the St.
    Bernard Hospice,
High up in the Alps near the pass of that
    name.
I was also sent out to rescue lost people.
It was this skill that soon earned me great
    fame.

The snow-covered mountains are spectacular
    but cruel;
Often, I've laboured through wide drifts of
    snow.
I've lost count of the numbers of people I've
    rescued.
But for me, the rewards are the best I could
    know.

These days, the search is often by helicopter,
My help isn't needed so much anymore.
The new teams are brilliant, but what
    people will miss
Is my smile, tots of brandy and a large
    friendly paw.

Saluki

I am tall and lanky. I'm just like my dear pet.
We both need daily walking, as much as we
    can get.
But while he strides with purpose, I dance
    upon my toes.
We cover many miles a day, as everyone
    local knows.
There are so many ways in which we
    resemble each other,
That after many years he's come to look
    more like a brother.

We both have thin and narrow faces,
    with a very pointed nose,
But neither sports moustaches. Perhaps
    that is why he chose
Me, a fair Saluki, to live with him for ever.
I, just like him, am both intelligent and
    clever.
So ours is the perfect partnership. We
    live in harmony.
Find a pet whom you resemble. Take a
    tip from me!

Schnautzer

My given name, you will have guessed, is
   German.
Which gives a hint of how I got that name.
The English translation of *schnautz* is snout,
(I prefer nose, which is almost the same).

I sport some magnificent moustaches,
Which cascade down both sides of my nose.
My stance is commanding; I always look
   noble,
Even when I'm stretched out, having a doze.

My ancestors go back for centuries.
While working for shepherds, they used to
   roam
The high pastures of Austria's Tyrol.
Austria remains my spiritual home.

But today, you'll find me all over the place.
I am a delightful family pet.
I am made in three different sizes.
So people can choose which model to get.

But it matters not which Schnauzer you have.
There are some attributes common to all:
Intelligence, friendliness, great sense of fun.
Once you have owned me, you'll be in my
thrall.

Sealyham Terrier

I was very popular, a hundred years ago.
You would see me everywhere and everyone
    would know
Exactly who I was. I used to love being on
    show.

But nowadays, you hardly see a Sealyham at
    all,
Which really is a tragedy. With my
    standing's fall,
I might disappear for ever, beyond anyone's
    recall.

I want to be sure you know something about
    me.
I come from Welsh Wales. My spirit is free.
My distinguished long nose is handsome to
    see.

My history is colourful, but I am quite
    white.
From a working farm terrier, I
    developed overnight
Into best friend to the famous, and I'm
    not yet out of sight.

Siberian Husky

My brothers and sisters were used to pull
   sleds,
Since time out of mind, it would seem.
We accompanied many intrepid explorers,
Obsessed with achieving their dream.

We are extraordinarily light on our feet.
Our handsome thick coats keep out Arctic
   cold.
Our teams cross the snow with comparative
   ease;
We work as a team, intrepid and bold.

We are perfectly made for these ventures;
Muscular, lean, we revel in speed.
But despite all our energy, we don't
Eat much; we are quite inexpensive to feed.

So, next time you're watching some
    programme
About famous explorers like Scott,
Please remember, without their brave
    Huskies,
They wouldn't have made it as far as they
    got.

Springer Spaniel

How I adore to play on the sand,
Not with a plastic bucket and spade.
No, my game involves racquet and ball.
It's the best game that I've ever played.

I bound joyfully off to the boundary,
This, the edge of the incoming tide,
I'm racing happily after a ball
That the man 'in' has hit very wide.

On the alert, feathered tail erect,
I attend when he's next taking aim.
I love my role as part of a team.
French Cricket's the name
   of the game.

Staffordshire Bull Terrier

I can really relate to those people
Whose reputations have bitten the dust,
Through the slanderous spreading of
    rumours,
By careless gossip that no-one should trust.

Sometimes it's a newspaper article
That begins the character's fall.
Or a tweet from some mischievous twit.
Or p'rhaps the source is not written at all.

Originally bred as a fighter,
Many long generations ago;
I am strong, tenacious and agile.
But here's something you may not know;

For years, I was favoured by miners in
    Durham,
Who'd families large and houses too small.
I would be left in charge of their offspring;
The parents could leave with no worries at
    all.

I used to be known as 'The Nanny Dog',
Though this term is now tarnished and
    rusty.
For all children, I always have had a soft
    spot.
I'm affectionate, loyal and trusty.

But because of my known fighting prowess,
Contemporary owners may want me to fight.
If provoked, or encouraged to do so,
Of course I will fight, with all of my might.

So, now, people think I'm ferocious;
These days I'm given a much wider berth.
But should you befriend a true 'Staffi', you'd
Find one of the kindest dogs on this earth.

Tyrolean Hound

In the Austrian Tyrol, where I come from,
The landscape's spectacular, the mountains
　　sublime.
For some of the year, it is covered with snow.
It is in this idyll that I spend my time.

I am a scent hound. I love to track creatures
Across the wide wastes of forests and
　　mountains.
I cannot imagine myself down in Salzburg,
Though I hear it is pretty, with elegant
　　fountains.

No, I am a hunter, and I am unique;
No other scent hound looks quite the same.
I'm lithe and compact. My coat's black or red.
The Tyrolean Hound is my proper name.

Victorian Bulldog

You've met my cousin, Winston.
Well, compared to him, I'm vast.
I tower above the lesser breed
Like a colossus from the past.

My face is covered in wrinkles.
My bandy legs stand wide.
My heavy jowls are pendulous.
I hold my head with pride.

Sophisticated breeding
Has produced the modern strain.
My origins, you will have guessed,
Date from Victoria's glorious reign.

Though I may look fearsome,
(My expression and my size),
I am the gentlest of canines,
Do not believe your eyes!

Weimaraner

I've an aloof, untouchable air,
From many years of contact with kings.
I was bred to hunt bear, deer and boar.
I don't bother myself with small things.

I am large and imposing, I'm stylish.
My short-haired coat is silvery grey.
Though my hunting with royals is over,
My demeanour still wins every day.

For I have won oodles of trophies,
My distinguished looks always admired.
I have often been judged best in show,
But I'm thinking it's time I retired.

For, though it is nice to win prizes,
I've had enough of circling the ring.
I am planning to write my memoirs,
Which I'm going to call '*Fit for a King*'.

Welsh Corgi

I will for ever be renowned
Because of being around
Our dear monarch, who was crowned
In 'fifty three,

For, throughout her glorious reign,
Until she said (this caused me pain)
She'd not have one of us again,
You'd always see

One, two, four or even more
Of us Welsh Corgis show a paw.
Not forced to follow any law,
Our lives were free.

Royal palaces, gardens, parks
All resounded to our barks.
We enjoyed our numerous larks
At royal knee.

Her Majesty, when at leisure,
In her Corgis took great pleasure.
Our head count is a measure;
Since 'fifty three,

More than thirty of our breed
Have kept our status up to speed,
To which no other will succeed.
Not after me.

But perhaps my crowning glory,
Was to appear in a Bond story
With the Queen; quite a furore.
Glory Be!

Whippet

I'm Queenie, a Whippet. I'm agile.
My torso, so slender, looks fragile,
But I'm tough as old boots!
See me when in cahoots
With my mates; I run mile after mile.

My small head is pointed and slim.
My figure is streamlined and trim.
I don't know whence I came.
I've been given this name.
My memories of childhood are dim.

A rescue dog I, from Battersea.
There, for months, nobody wanted me.
I was found on the street
With poor damaged feet,
My rough, mangy coat sad to see.

Now I'm restored, I'm happy to say,
My beautiful coat's a silky grey.
I can dance on my toes,
So not anyone knows
How I came to my pets, where I'll stay.

Xolocuintal

I have to be included here
For my name starts with an X.
No other dog can boast of that.
This muscle I like to flex!

I'm a cheerful, intelligent dog,
I may or may not have hair.
Though I am made in three sizes,
I'm afraid sightings of me are rare.

I originally came from Mexico,
Part of an ancient Aztec line.
But you'll have to take my word
For it that Xolocuintals are divine!

Yorkshire Terrier

I look more like a toy than a terrier.
I am small and very pretty, you see.
But beneath my hair, so carefully coiffed,
You will very quickly find the real me.

I have a sharp, high, repetitive bark,
Which I practise as often as I can.
For though my size may be diminutive,
With my yap I've scared many a man.

I am also a very practised ankle-biter.
One great bonus of being so small
Is that a man's ankle is just the right height;
I can nip it while hardly moving at all.

But, of course, I don't go for everyone.
Most of the time I'm delightfully sweet;
Pretty and playful, I'll be your best friend,
As long as I get my favourite treat.

Zuchon

I am so delighted to be meeting you all
    again,
By virtue of the fact that my name begins
    with 'Z'.
You have met me as a show dog, which
    indeed I am,
But I'm sure you're not aware of my 'street
    cred.'.

For I can charm myself into almost
    anywhere,
From Claridges in Mayfair to Ronnie's in
    Soho.
Because I am so pretty, I have always been
    a star.
People will acknowledge me, wherever I
    may go.

It is a pleasure to break out of the show-
    ring,
I love making an entrance, I relish
    applause.
My appearance is stellar. I've glamour
    and polish
From my stylish *coiffure* to the nails on
    my paws.

Postscript

I am so very much more than a pet;
I am your confidant. I know your soul.
You'll never shock me, for I never judge.
I am a healer. I help make you whole.
When life's dealing blows which are
　　crushing,
I give you comfort and soothe your frayed
　　nerves.
My paw on your foot is showing you love,
Surely, such love each human deserves.

Other Works by Gill Rowe

Pirouetting Hippos

'Hugely entertaining'.
'Quite unique'.
'As I read I chuckle often and marvel at your insights into life, persons, places and things'.

How Do I Look?

'So fresh and original'.
'I love your new book – so true to life and it makes me laugh'.
'You have exactly caught the current climate and mores in verse'.

You're Telling Me!

'Your poems not only bring a smile, they reach out to people with endearing warmth'.
'Full of perceptive capturing of life. To see humour in the commonplace, as you do, is delightful'.

'The poems contain much wisdom in a very entertaining packaging!'.

Widening Horizons

'I admire your ability to express so aptly what you have observed so keenly'.
'Your reflections lifted my spirits and took me to a better place'.
'I really admire your ability to combine lightness of touch and playfulness with reflection'.

A Whiff of Rosemary

'I loved your poetry'.
'Congratulations on another wise and witty volume'.
'You seize the incidents of life which we all recognise and experience and reproduce them to comic – and touching – effect. More please!'.

Stalking the Crilbit

'beautifully clever and crafted verse'.
'Loved your very intelligent and witty poems'.
'glorious poems'.

Tails You Win

'If you are a dog lover you will love this
book of poems'.
'Perfect fun gift for any dog lover!'.
'Quick and entertaining'.
'If you are a dog fan, then I absolutely
recommend that you read this book'.
'This was such a lovely read. I'd recommend
it to anyone who loves dogs like I do. It will
stand up to repeat readings, and I look forward
to dipping back in again in the future'.